Public Speaking

90 Minute Guides

Michelle N. Halsey

Silver City Publications & Training, L.L.C.
P.O. Box 1914
Nampa, ID 83653
https://www.silvercitypublications.com/shop/

ISBN-10: 1-64004-034-X
ISBN-13: 978-1-64004-034-2

Contents

Chapter 1 – Identifying Your Audience

According to a survey by the Sunday Times of London, 41% of people list public speaking as their biggest fear. Forget small spaces, darkness, and spiders – standing up in front of a crowd and talking is far more terrifying for most people.

However, mastering this fear and getting comfortable speaking in public can be a great ego booster, not to mention a huge benefit to your career. This workshop will give you some valuable public speaking skills, including in-depth information on developing an engaging program and delivering your presentation with power.

By the end of this chapter, you will be able to:

- Identify their audience

- Create a basic outline

- Organize their ideas

- Flesh out their presentation

- Find the right words

- Prepare all the details

- Overcome nervousness

- Deliver a polished, professional speech

- Handle questions and comments effectively

Think about the most effective presentation or speech you have ever heard. Keep it in mind while reading the chapter to help identify practical applications for the tools and techniques that we discuss.

Identifying Your Audience

The key to effective public speaking is preparation. The better you prepare, the more confident you will feel.

Preparation begins with identifying your audience. What do you know about your audience? What do they care about? What's important to them? Do they have any misconceptions about your topic? These are the kinds of questions you should ask as part of your preparation. Sitting down and listing the questions, and your answers to them, will give you a basic structure for your speech, around which you can add things and take them away as you see fit.

Holding the attention of an audience and speaking to what interests them is the most important thing about any public speech. It is not merely about what you say, but also how you say it. If you have a message you wish to get across, then think of how that message will communicate itself best to the audience you are speaking to.

Performing a Needs Analysis

Preparing for a speech should begin with thinking about the wants and needs of the audience. What are they interested in? What do they care about? No matter how entertaining a speaker you are, people will not give you their full attention unless you are talking about something that is meaningful to them.

You should try to let the audience know early in your speech that you are going to try to address their concerns. Too often a speaker starts out with a lengthy discussion about the history or background of a topic. That is usually not what the audience cares about! They want to know how this topic will affect their lives.

A needs analysis measures what skills employees have -- and what they need. It indicates how to deliver the right training at the right time. The results answer the following questions:

- Where is the *audience* with the problem or need for change?

- What *tasks* and subtasks does an expert perform to complete a work process?

- What *gaps* exist between experts, average, and poor performers of a work process?

- How do we translate the needs into objectives to promote a strong learning *outcome*?

The method can be simple observation, careful note taking, and asking questions.

Question	Methods
Audience?	Interview key stakeholders and listen to their concerns about the problem Define who needs help to overcome the problem Identify and describe the audience and the work
Tasks?	Observe the work being done by recognized experts Take careful notes and ask questions where needed Document the proper performance of the work tasks
Gaps?	Observe other workers doing the tasks. Compare results with the performance of experts. Document identified skill gaps.
Outcome?	Develop a complete list of tasks for performing the work completely and correctly.

Creating an Audience Profile

- **Education:** If your audience is well-educated, you can use fairly sophisticated vocabulary. If they're not, you need to keep things simple.

- **Familiarity with Topic:** What do people know about the topic already and what do you need to explain?

- **Familiarity with Jargon:** Avoid any specialized vocabulary unless you think that everyone in the audience will understand it. If you have to use a technical term, explain it.

- **Interest in the Topic:** What do people care about? What's important to them?

- **Possible Misconceptions:** Which incorrect ideas might you need to correct?

- **Attitude:** Are people hostile, supportive, curious, worried? The attitude of your audience will affect the tone of your speech.

One of the most important elements of written or spoken language is the register in which it is delivered. Experts say that there are three registers of language, titled R1, R2, and R3. R1 is the level of language used most commonly by politicians, lawyers, and found in the upper-market range of newspapers. R2 is the most commonly used by people in everyday conversation with acquaintances and people they have just met (outside a framework of formality).

R3 is the register that may be used between close friends and is heavily based in slang. Considering how educated your audience is, and how formal you wish the speech to be, will govern the choice of register.

The audience's familiarity with an interest in the topic will also be of importance. You may be seeking to educate your audience on the topic in hand, or to communicate your own ideas to an audience who is already familiar with the topic. Deciding between these will help shape your speech – if they are familiar with the topic then it does not hurt to include some jargon, as this may even make your speech that little bit more dynamic – if you don't need to keep explaining things, you can communicate ideas more effectively.

The mood and opinion of your audience is also important. It will influence the tone and content of your speech, as a nervous or worried audience will require an element of comfort or reassurance, while a celebratory audience will want to share a positive, electric atmosphere and possibly hear some congratulations.

One person speaking to a large crowd is in a unique position – they have the attention of many people and the power to get ideas across that will change mindsets and behavior on a large scale. It is therefore important to consider how you phrase things, and that you correct any persistent misconceptions of which you are aware.

Identifying Key Questions and Concerns

If you have a good understanding of your audience, you can probably predict the key questions and concerns they are likely to have. You may not be able to give the audience the answers they would like to hear, but at least you should be ready to discuss the things they care about most.

Many speeches these days are followed by a question and answer session which allows the audience to raise any issues they do not feel have been fully dealt with by the original speech – but it is better for the audience if the original speech deals with those concerns, as it shows that they have been thought through rather than addressed "on the hoof".

Predicting questions and concerns should be straightforward. If you are in a position to address a larger group of people, then the chances are that you have knowledge of the issues that affect them and how these can be addressed. It is also possible to take a sounding from people "on the ground" as to what is concerning them. It may well be that you share those concerns and have given some thought to addressing them.

If you can speak intelligently and emotionally about the issues that concern your audience, they will have a lot more trust that you can help provide solutions to problems, and that their position is understood and respected.

It may help before delivering a speech or presentation to make a list of the five most searching questions you expect people to have. Your presentation should then concern itself with answering those questions as well as delivering your own standpoint.

When delivering the speech it is helpful to pay tribute to the fact that these concerns exist, by saying something along the lines of: "And before I go any further, I would like to raise an issue that I know has been foremost among the minds of many here…". As the audience is giving you their attention, it is simply reasonable that you make clear that they, too, have yours.

Creating a Basic Outline

The main advantage of creating an outline is that it helps you to organize your thoughts. The audience gets more out of a presentation when it is well-organized. They also are more likely to think that the speaker knows the subject thoroughly and has given some thought on how to present it.

In this module we will be considering a hypothetical presentation about a project that has just been completed, but the general approach we will consider is applicable to just about any type of presentation.

Often this approach is seen as being similar to creating a body. You start with the skeleton – the basic outline, the bare minimum of the speech in something like the shape that it will eventually take – and progress by adding meat to the bones, and layering the rest on top of that.

At key points of the presentation, specific issues will need to be confronted, and by allotting them a place in the basic outline you will be able to ensure that these are prioritized and addressed correctly.

Outlining the Situation

Almost every project addresses a problem, an opportunity, or both. An effective way to introduce your speech is by outlining the situation that your project addresses. This approach forces you to get to the point right away.

In outlining the situation, try to avoid giving too much history or background. Most people won't care about that sort of information. If you start out by discussing something people don't care about, it will be hard to recapture their interest.

Provide only the background information people will need to understand the situation. Your audience in many cases may already know the background. Covering old ground will simply lead to a "here we go again" feeling in the room.

So instead of beginning with a history of the problem, the nature of the problem can be covered in a few sentences, and followed with a statement of what you as a group decided had to be done about it. It is beneficial to make reference to situations and occasions with which the audience is familiar. In doing this you will keep their attention by recognizing that their opinions mattered and were taken into account.

The introduction of a presentation is where you will often take and hold an audience's attention, or lose it for good. It is wise, then, to keep an introduction brief and informative, and set the scene for the rest of the presentation.

In an introduction, there are just a few essential elements to keep in mind. First of all, you should introduce yourself in your capacity with regards to the project. Even if everyone there knows you, it helps to explain exactly why *you* are delivering the presentation. You should then give a brief overview of what the presentation seeks to address.

This will stop anyone in the audience from thinking "When are they going to get to the bit about *x*?", and allow all present to concentrate on the presentation itself.

Identifying the Task That Had to Be Performed

Your task description will be the organizing principle for the rest of your presentation. Most of what follows will be an account of what you did to complete the task.

One way to come up with a simple, clear task description is to imagine you are writing it for a teenager. How would you describe what you did to someone who knows very little about your work? This can obviously be tweaked depending on the audience, but it is worthwhile remembering that the audience to which you speak will all have their specialties in certain fields. Something that is perfectly evident to you may not be perfectly evident to many in your audience.

This does not mean that a lot of your speech should be taken up by lengthy explanations of what you do. Think of it in a similar way to a film. In most films we have periods of what the directors like to call "exposition". They lay down the "back story", telling us why what we are watching had to happen.

Film reviewers are very quick to criticize films which have lengthy spells of exposition, as all we really need are the essential details. We can piece the rest together for ourselves. Take the same approach to explaining the task that you were dealing with. Give the important details, and assume a basic level of understanding.

The result of having these brief explanations is that your wider presentation will then be set in a certain context, and it is in this context where the things you say will make sense. When you have completed the first draft of the presentation or speech it helps to then read over it and see if it would make sense to someone who is coming to the presentation without the information that you have.

Any terms which give space for confusion can then be explained a little bit better so that the audience can follow the presentation. If any remaining confusion persists, then a question-and-answer period can pick that up.

Listing the Actions You Took

If a presentation contains a list of actions, it's a good idea to present the list on a slide or a flip chart. People have a hard time keeping more than three or four items straight in their head unless they see them displayed.

As you go through your list in your presentation, you can point to each item on your chart or slide. This will make it easier for people to follow along. It will also help people see where you are in your presentation, and how much longer it is likely to go on.

It is important to do this for a number of reasons:

- Firstly, if people are confused as to what exactly will be dealt with – and when – they are liable to lose concentration, and any key points you make in the presentation will resonate less as a result of people wondering what is next.

- Secondly, there will be people in your audience who, although they are keen to listen closely to the presentation, will still wonder when their particular area of interest will be dealt with. We change how we listen depending on our familiarity with the topic.

- Thirdly, if people are concerned about the length of the presentation, their minds will begin to wander as it passes the point where they would have hoped for it to finish.

Making the audience aware of the structure of your presentation in advance may seem to some like an invitation for them to tune in and tune out as the topics suit. However, having a table of contents allows people to keep concentration.

In the areas where they are less informed than in others, they will listen in order to further inform themselves. In their areas of expertise they will listen not more closely, but differently – giving themselves a chance to contribute after the presentation if necessary.

A good structure does not just help the writer and deliverer of a presentation, but the audience too. It is easier to maintain concentration if one is aware of what they should be concentrating on and this will mean that you carry the audience with you over the course of your presentation, allowing them to be better informed, reassured, and prepared at the end of your presentation than they were at the beginning.

Revealing the Results

Revealing the results of a project involves answering a few basic questions:

- Did the project achieve its goal?

- Were there any unexpected consequences?

- What's next?

The first question may seem like an obvious one with an obvious answer. Simply put, either it achieved its objective or it did not. However, any project will have stages of success and stages of failure. In deciding whether a project achieved its goal it is important to refer back to the questions and the brief as set out in the introduction to the presentation.

There was a plan to achieve something – did it succeed? If so, did it come through on, or ahead of, schedule? Was any outside help required? And if it failed, did it fall some distance short or was it close enough to be termed a "deferment" rather than a straight failure?

As for unexpected consequences, these can arise in any project. In preparation for a project, it is common to look ahead at potential problems and decide how these can be avoided or addressed. However, the best laid plans can still always run up against unforeseen problems – and, for that matter, unforeseen benefits.

These can change the shape of a project and lead to the redrawing of an entire brief. Often the kind of on-the-spot management that is required to handle such a situation can be the difference between success and failure, and any conclusion should deal with these circumstances, how they arose, and how they were dealt with.

At the end of the presentation, it is safe to say that the audience will be better informed as to the extent of the success or failure of a plan. Their minds will then, naturally, turn to the matter of where things will go next. Assuming that the business itself has not been wound up, there will be follow-up work to do, and getting on with that work will be the priority.

The question of "What next?" can be answered with reference to the presentation you have just delivered. Everyone will now be clearer on the consequences of the previous months, and now is the best time to lay down the next plan.

Chapter 2 – Organizing the Program

The key to creating a well-organized speech or presentation is to keep your audience in mind. Start with something that will capture their attention and give them a clear idea of your topic.

Organize the body of your presentation in a way that will be easy for your audience to understand. Plan to review your main points briefly and then wrap things up on a positive note, perhaps giving your audience a "call to action."

The essential thing to remember is that you are giving your presentation for the benefit of your audience. That means you need to organize it in a way that will make sense to them. The most important thing to keep in the forefront of your mind is that you are not making the speech for yourself, but your audience.

Think of how politicians do things. When they are campaigning they will speak to groups as diverse as different occupations, different ethnicities, and different ages. How they will speak to each changes between speeches. Then, when they are speaking to a cabinet meeting of fellow politicians, the language and the issues will be different again. Keep this in mind when giving a presentation.

Making Organization Easy

Some thoughts on the basic parts of a presentation:

Opening. Some speakers like to start a presentation with a joke. Sometimes this works. It starts on a light note and puts the audience at ease. Buy many people do not tell jokes well. If a presentation starts with something that doesn't work, the audience will start to question your ability as a speaker. Other ways to start include asking a rhetorical question, giving people a surprising statistic, or telling a brief anecdote that is related to the topic of the presentation.

Body. The next two activities will address the body of a presentation.

Review. Many speakers skip this step, but it can be worth including. Chances are that some members of the audience didn't get the few key points you want them to take away from the presentation. Restate these key points briefly for the sake of those who were "tuned out" the first time you made them.

Closing. Restate the main point of your presentation. In some cases, you may want to give people a "call to action."

Obviously, the longer a presentation goes on the more chances there are to lose the attention of your audience. However, making a presentation too short can leave people uninformed and dissatisfied with the body of the presentation. It is therefore essential to structure your presentation correctly, allowing enough time to give it a powerful opening which will draw listeners in, a strong middle which will hold that attention and give them all the facts, and a closing section which reinforces what they were told and gives them an idea about what action needs to be taken to back it all up.

All these parts need to be present, and each needs to be weighted correctly according to the amount of time you have available to you. It may well be the case that in order to attend a presentation people are taken away from doing their "normal" job.

Such demands on a person's time will reflect in how they view the presentation and how much of their attention they give it.

The amount of time you give to each section of a presentation will therefore be governed by how much time you have overall and how much of that time will be necessary to get all of your substantive points across. If your presentation is in danger of running over time, it will be necessary to trim it in places, beginning with any extraneous detail.

Remember that most presentations will be followed up by a pick-up session of sorts, where individual questions can be dealt with. The presentation itself is where larger issues are raised and answered.

Organizational Methods

It's important to realize that most people will be able to remember only a few key points from a presentation. Don't overwhelm the audience with facts that they will forget as soon as they walk out the door. Focus on a few key points.

It's a good idea to write your key points on a flip chart or show them on a slide. That will help your audience understand how your presentation is organized. If you return to your flip chart page or slide when you move on to a new key point, the audience will be able to see where you are in your presentation.

As well as this, at the close of a presentation you can then go, one by one, through the key points that you have made. Making a point coherently consists of three steps: introduction, substance, and reinforcement. If you want the audience to leave your presentation with a certain point locked in their minds, then it is essential that you address all three of those steps.

Whichever way you choose to organize the body of your presentation, it is important to keep the elements of it down to a manageable number. Taking one of the above as an example, we will look at how a "Problem/Solution" style of presentation can best be cut down into a few manageable steps.

An organization may have any number of problems which it wishes to address. If there are, say, fifteen problems that it wants to get to the bottom of it, covering all of these in a presentation results in the problem that fifteen of anything is a large number to remember.

In order to ensure that the presentation does not result in an audience being bemused by the sheer number of problems, it is advisable if you can to find a category for each problem, whether it be "time", "manpower", "finance" or another suitable category.

Your intention should be to find a few category headings which can cover a few problems each. If these problems require more time, this can best be covered by a meeting where the attendees are all people who have experience in the specific field where problems exist.

Any presentation will benefit from this kind of organization. One thing worth remembering is that the "rule of three" is adhered to by most people, if not consciously then certainly subconsciously. Therefore if you can keep concentrated discussion to around three headings – or a maximum of five – then you will be able to retain attention much better than if you have a numbered list which never seems to end. You can always, after all, emphasize the key points at the end of the presentation.

Classifying and Categorizing

Categorizing information is one way that people make sense of complex topics. A speaker can help people come to grips with complex topics by breaking them down into a few categories.

If participants have trouble thinking of things to consider in a health insurance plan, you can make a few suggestions:

Cost:

- Payroll deductions
- Copayments
- Cost of prescriptions

Coverage:

- Hospitalization
- Emergency room visits
- Coverage when traveling
- Annual physicals
- Routine doctor's visits

Choice:

- Referral requirements
- Network restrictions (doctors)
- Network restrictions (hospitals)

One key benefit of doing this is that you can take a highly complicated topic and break it down into smaller areas, which benefits members of your audience who may specialize in a certain area. The areas in which they do not specialize will not be a signal to turn off, but an opportunity to learn more about that specific area, allowing a "joined-up" process to have greater success within the organization. The areas in which they do specialize are an opportunity for them to listen, evaluate, and potentially contribute suggestions which may benefit everyone in future.

Additionally, the introduction of smaller topic areas allows the brain to process information in more manageable "chunks". Rather than trying to make sense of a topic which seems monolithic in size and importance, cutting it down into smaller pieces allows the individual to mentally breathe in between those sections.

Think of it as being like a journey. If you were to travel from one tip of Africa to the other in one go, you would be exhausted and unwell at the end of it. If, on the other hand, you include stopping-off points and rest breaks, you will allow yourself to recover and galvanize yourself for the journey ahead.

This approach applies in the healthcare example detailed above, but also in several other areas. A broader topic can be split down into more specific topics, which in themselves can potentially be split into more, even hyper-specific areas depending upon the audience you are dealing with. It is also essential not to overdo this.

By splitting down a topic repeatedly you can end up with so many chunks that the constant changing leads to a presentation losing its momentum. A balance between over-complication and over-simplification is essential. If you get it right in the middle, the presentation will flow naturally.

Fleshing It Out

Audiences are often a little skeptical about a speaker's message, especially if the speaker is addressing a controversial issue. You can build credibility with an audience by using reliable sources of information and backing up your statements with citations to trusted authorities.

You need to think about your presentation as though it was going to be written down on paper and distributed throughout the audience and their bosses. Throwaway lines which you assumed would just pass over people's heads will end up being the bits that certain people remember – so be sure to keep a close eye on what you say and how you say it.

Often, people make the mistake of believing that the more they say, the better their speech is. Others, feeling that brevity is the soul of wit, keep what they say to a minimum. As with so many things, the truth lies somewhere in between and the key to making a presentation as powerful and as well-received as it can be is to say enough, and make what you say mean enough.

There is no point in fleshing out a presentation with extraneous detail which no-one will remember, and at the same time you should avoid leaving out anything remotely important so that your message is strong, coherent, and memorable.

Chapter 3 – Identifying Appropriate Sources

The Internet supplies us with an endless stream of information, but how reliable is it? One way to evaluate reliability is to compare data from several different sources. One way to check for bias (especially with controversial topics) is to compare statements by people who have opposing views.

For people who wish their words to be given attention and taken seriously, balance is of vital importance. Maintaining that balance relies on good research and not allowing your opinion to be mistaken in your mind for fact. There is so much information available for research, and your task is to separate the redundant, excess information from the important data.

For example, many people use the popular online encyclopedia Wikipedia for research. This is not a bad idea; the site is filled with information which is well cross-referenced and constantly updated. In terms of freshness, online encyclopedias such as this cannot be beaten by the traditional, paper-based form of encyclopedia, which in turn are incredibly inconvenient for the purposes of cross-reference. So if there is this much convenience to an online encyclopedia, and so much information therein, we should be looking to use it for all of our research needs, should we not?

Well, in fairness, using an online resource like Wikipedia can be a very good way to do substantial research, but it is important to make sure that any facts and figures you use from a Wikipedia article are cited and backed up by other sources.

You will find the citation reference in square brackets next to the information in the article body. This links to the table of references, which can be used to find the source that, the statistics or other information were drawn from. The more sources you have for information – and the more views you listen to from both sides of a debate – the better for any research that you do. Even if you disagree with the information and opinions given by a certain source, it can after all be used as a jumping-off point for a counter-argument.

Establishing Credibility

It is extremely important to be sure of your facts. If you make even one factually incorrect statement, some people will doubt everything you say. This is something that holds true wherever you are, including in some of the highest courts in the land.

A lawyer will be much in demand if he or she can take one small inaccuracy in a witness' statement and turn it to the advantage of his or her client by using it to paint the witness as unreliable. In terms of a presentation, the stakes may not be as high, but all the same it is wise to make sure that you have authority behind what you tell people. This begins with how you present yourself.

It is often said that you cannot judge a book by its cover, and the truth is that that it absolutely correct. Some fine minds are to be found behind faces which appear, to many people to suggest docility.

But if you want to keep the audience's attention on what you are saying, it is advisable to appear businesslike and efficient at all times. You should be tidily dressed, and should be aware at all times of what you have just said, what you are currently saying, and what you will say next. If this involves referring to flash cards on occasion, then there is no problem in doing so – much better to have the information to hand than have it disappear from your mind.

It is also worth bearing in mind the fact that the audience have not come to be told things they already know. If they had, then any one of them could be giving the presentation. It is much better to think about things from another angle.

You know what they think, so some of this presentation can be about what you think. The bits of the presentation that they remember may well be the moments when their opinions were challenged and potentially changed. Doing this will involve arguing a point and backing it up with sound reasoning, facts and figures, and the impact it has on an audience can be genuinely impressive.

You should use whatever is at your disposal to make your points in a presentation as efficiently as possible. Known statistics, testimonies from respected individuals and documentary evidence are all extremely helpful when it comes to making your point effectively.

Each person in the audience may have a different "convincer". The more complete your presentation is, the more people you will convince. Unless you are preaching to the converted, do not assume that you will carry all before you with the same arguments that sounded right to you.

The Importance of Citations

Some groups or individuals are so trusted that citing their statements can be the deciding factor in getting people to agree with you. Some examples:

- The Centers for Disease Control

- The Congressional Budget Office

- The Census Bureau

- The Journal of the American Medical Association

The point that unites these groups listed above, and others like them, is that they are considered to be a leading authority in their specific field. When it comes to discovering information on any subject, going right to the leading authorities to find it out is always a sensible move.

If you are giving a presentation, going to a leading authority in the area you wish to discuss is very wise indeed. Sometimes in a presentation you will find that some of your listeners are skeptical and will challenge the statistics you mention. If you can mention that those statistics have come from a leading authority, and cite that they are up to date as well, then you will advance your case much further.

It has become common practice to begin sentences in presentations, essays and speeches with the phrase "Everybody knows that…" or "It goes without saying that…" when often this is very far from being the case.

This is a rhetorical device which can be used appropriately and inappropriately. In the first case, if it is something everyone does know, then it prevents you from having to go over well-worn explanations. In many other cases, however, it may be used because the speaker has not been able to source direct proof for an assertion and simply wants their audience to accept it. After all, if "everybody" knows something, not many people will happily be the one to disagree.

When it comes to backing your points up, it is best that you go to the experts.

The more evidence you can back up a statement with, the more confidence you can have in asserting it. Furthermore, the fact that the information comes from a trusted source means that you can immediately trump skeptical listeners who wish to make your presentation seem less informed than it is.

Putting It All Together

Once you've outlined your speech and lined up some solid evidence to back up your ideas, it's time to put all the pieces together. Whether you plan to write out your speech word for word or just speak from notes, you need to have a clear idea of what you want to say — the actual words, not just the ideas.

It is generally recommended not to have everything you want to say written down but rather a series of prompts. If you appear to be reading from a script, then there is less chance of you getting your point across with the power that you want it to have.

Nonetheless, you should refrain from improvising too much as there are clear disadvantages to this process, not least of them the fact that this is filled with risks such as momentarily being lost for words.

This makes you appear less competent, and people will be less likely to take you seriously. The general impression is that you should have in mind the body of what you want to say, and any additions which occur to you can always be included. Therefore, you do not have to worry about deviating from a pre-written speech, while also avoiding the dangers of having nothing to say.

Chapter 4 – Writing Your Presentation

Most of the time it's a bad idea to read a presentation word for word. It's boring and it makes it difficult to build a rapport with the audience. Any presentation is a kind of social occasion. If you just wanted people to hear what you have to say, you could print copies of your presentation and hand them out.

Effective speakers try to make a connection with their audience. Reading a speech word for word creates a barrier between the speaker and the audience and eliminates spontaneity. Your audience should feel like you're having a conversation with them, not lecturing them.

If you are constantly referring to notes this makes it impossible to maintain any kind of eye contact with your audience, and you may as well record the speech and play it to them. Speaking from notes does not have the same problems connected with it – it simply allows you to have prompts from which to elaborate.

The main benefit to making a speech is that you allow your words to come alive. Some of the most impressive speeches are made by speakers who have minimal notes and have thought long and hard about what they want to say and how they want to say it. This allows them to maintain a rapport with their audience, and gives the words more resonance. Also, if you are reading from a full speech, this makes it more difficult to respond to questions which may arise in the course of your presentation. Allowing your brain to do most of the work sharpens your reaction times and gives you greater credibility.

If you wish to write out any part of your speech or memorize it word for word, the best thing to do is write down what you will say in the first two or three minutes of the speech. From here you can usually gain the confidence that you require to give the rest of your speech more freely. By this point, you will have gained the confidence of your audience, who will be happy to hear what you have to say, and you will be "warmed up" – making the rest of the speech far more coherent and convincing.

Adding a Plan B

It is almost inevitable that at some point you will encounter unexpected problems in giving presentations. How you handle these problems, will determine whether your presentation is a success or not.

Some people get very flustered when something goes wrong. They may become irritated or angry. The audience picks up on this emotion and starts to form a negative impression of the speaker. Skillful speakers treat unexpected problems humorously. If their projector doesn't work or they trip over a cord, they make a joke out of it.

This puts everyone at ease and starts to build a rapport with the audience. This is one element which separates comfortable public speakers from speakers who are less professional.

The importance of having a Plan B is recognized by everyone who has a Plan A. The thing that many people forget about plans is that they are not always going to be carried out in the conditions for which they were planned.

Things can go wrong without notice. Even if you have planned out every seemingly foreseeable eventuality there is always the danger that, for example, the power will go off in the middle of the presentation. How you react to these problems is almost as important as the quality of your speech.

Good public speakers will always be ready for the possibility of unforeseen problems. This does not mean that, should you spill something over your notes or have a momentary lapse of memory, you should launch into a stand-up comedy routine. It is much better to simply go into the speech you have planned with the awareness that you may need to "fill space". One way in which people do this is to make light of the problem and – if you can think of a way to do so – make the unexpected problem into part of your Plan B.

For example – and this is a very specific example – if the power should cut out during a speech on the importance of energy efficiency, you can turn this into a jumping off point by saying "…and this is a good example of the importance of what I am talking about. Thank you very much for that illustration". Of course, sometimes the fates will throw problems at you that are not so easily turned into a joke, but thinking on your feet will win you points.

Often, it is enough simply to know that you may encounter such problems and to have an attitude those things are in the lap of the gods. Having the confidence to turn them into something that can drive a presentation forward is the mark of a good speaker.

Reviewing, Editing, and Rewriting

Here are some things to look for in reviewing the first draft of a presentation:

Content and Organization:

- Does the opening provide a good idea of what the presentation is about?

- Are the main ideas arranged in a logical order?

- Are opinions backed up with facts, statistics, and authorities?

Language:

- Have you come with clear, effective statements of your main ideas?

- Have you eliminated jargon as much as possible?

- Have you used vocabulary that the audience will understand?

Length:

- Have you devoted an appropriate amount of time to each part of your presentation?

- Is your entire presentation an appropriate length?

Very few first drafts are good enough to be "the draft". Unless you have immense clarity of thought and eerie foresight, the chances are that you will make a reference later on in your speech that either contradicts something you said before, or has a meaning that is not immediately clear to your listeners going on the basis of what you said before.

The first draft of a speech is about getting all your ideas on to the page and ensuring that they are coherently presented. The further drafts will be about ensuring that the speech flows like it should, and sounds like a complete document rather than a series of thoughts.

Writing a speech that takes all of the important factors into account first time is not impossible, but does take an inordinate period of time, and the final document can often sound like pages of research.

Getting the balance right between informative content and something that will hold the attention of your audience generally requires you to revisit the speech after you have written it. You could sit to write with a reference book in front of you, checking every fact, figure and quote before you commit it to paper. However, this approach almost always leads to a speech that has very little life in it.

The best bet is to write a draft of the speech that sounds like something you would say. The latter drafts of it will then take into account the details that you have checked, and any amendments you have made as a result of a read-through.

It may be that in the original draft you have given more time to one section than you have to another, equally important section. By adding and subtracting elements, you will have a speech that sounds coherent and impressive. By sitting and working on a first draft that takes everything into account and has all of the important facts and figures checked, you will have a speech that sounds like a research document.

Chapter 5 – Being Prepared

Preparation serves several important purposes:

- It boosts your self-confidence.

- It reduces the chances of something going wrong.

- It creates an impression of you as a competent, diligent person.

- It makes it easier for you to give a polished, professional presentation.

It is often said that those who fail to prepare, prepare to fail. The reason for this is that only by preparing properly will you eliminate the obvious potential errors that can turn what would be an excellent speech into a mess.

By taking the time to prepare, you can look ahead to the presentation and get an impression for how it should and will go. It will also allow you to take into consideration what difficulties may arise, and have a strategy for dealing with each of them.

Some people can walk into a room and hold the attention of their audience by speaking "off the cuff" for half an hour or more. These people are naturally gifted, and quite rare. Usually, they make a living as stand-up comedians, as comedy is one of very few fields where the act of preparing a routine is not hamstrung by the necessity for getting every fact right and every detail nailed down.

This does not mean that delivering a presentation cannot be an enjoyable process. In fact, the right amount and the right kind of preparation can ensure that the presentation is enjoyable, informative, and useful both for you and for your audience.

Checking Out the Venue

Here are some things to look for when checking out the venue for a presentation:

- Adequate seating.

- Good sight lines. Some chairs may need to be moved so that everyone can see the speaker or the screen.

- Projectors or other equipment. If you will be using the site's projector, be sure it works, and check to see if it is compatible with your laptop. Will you need an extension cord?

- Lighting. What combination of lights will allow the audience to see you, their notes, and the screen if you plan to use slides?

- Speaker's accommodations. Is there a podium if you plan to use one? Is there a place for you to put handouts?

- Miscellaneous. Where are the restrooms and emergency exits?

Sometimes a lot of preparation goes into a presentation, taking into account the way the speaker moves, sounds and sees the audience, as well as the visual aids the speaker will use during the course of the presentation.

A great deal of preparation should ensure that things go smoothly, but the level of presentation needs to be matched by the quality of preparation. Think for a moment how you would react if you had written a 30-minute presentation which called for frequent reference to a visual slideshow, and when you arrived at the venue you found that they did not have a projector.

If you can have access to the venue before you deliver the presentation, this should allow you to carry out a study of the room and get all the information you need. If you can have access for long enough to do a "dry run", so much the better, as this will allow you to foresee any problems and either amend your speech or make alternative arrangements.

It is essential that you take nothing for granted when seeking to deliver a presentation, because it will be you who is in the unenviable position of explaining and dealing with any problems that happen during the live presentation.

If you cannot get access to the venue prior to your presentation, then you should at least be able to get a floor plan of the venue and a checklist of items you will have available to you, as well as knowing whether the venue will support any equipment you bring with you.

If you have written into your presentation a very clever ten-minute scenario that requires you to walk among the audience, you will need to know that the layout of the room allows this. If you have included a short film in your presentation, it will be entirely useless if most people cannot see the film because a pillar is in their way.

Then, before you deliver your presentation, you should look around the room and ensure that nothing there will distract people from what you are saying, and visualize how you will deliver your speech in this room.

Gathering Materials

If you are going to use handouts, be sure you have enough. Handouts serve several purposes:

- Listeners like to take notes. Listeners like to have something to take away from your presentation as a reminder of what you said. Many listeners will take notes on any scrap of paper that is handy. By providing your listeners with handouts, you can reduce the time they spend taking notes because they will already have the main information you are presenting.

- The less time they spend taking notes, the more time they can spend focusing on you.

- Handouts help reinforce your main points. People listen selectively. As hard as you try to emphasize a particular point, some listeners will remember some other point you made that was probably less important. Handouts will help you drive home your main message.

- Handouts make listeners happy. People like to take away something tangible from a presentation, something more than their recollection of what you said. Giving people handouts makes them feel as if they "own" the information they have just heard.

When you write your speech, it is beneficial to condense what you are saying into its key points. This is beneficial for the sake of having visual prompts for what you are going to say, but can actually serve a dual purpose. If you condense a speech into its key points and other useful information, then in this form or in a slightly amended one it can make an excellent handout.

As wonderful as your speech may be, remember that it will be experienced slightly differently by however many people hear it. All of these people may take something slightly different away from the room, so if you have absolutely concrete points that you would insist on them remembering, ensure that these are available on the handout.

By giving everyone a handout you also ensure that they feel as though they have participated in the presentation. Rather than simply demanding that they sit there, listen and remember everything you have said, you give them what is in effect a souvenir of the occasion (in fact, *souvenir* is by origin a French word for "to remember").

This will be something they can refer back to after the event, particularly if they annotate the handout themselves with their own thoughts or something specific that you said during the presentation. Additionally, this allows them to sit and listen to the presentation as you deliver it, without having to constantly write and refer back to detailed notes during the speech.

Chapter 6 – A 24-Hour Checklist

Presentation:

___ Do you know what you're going to say in the first two minutes?

___ Do you know how you're going to introduce your topic?

___ Have you prepared clear statements of your main points?

___ Do you know how you're going to close your presentation?

___ Have you prepared answers for the questions that are likely to come up?

Slides and handouts:

___ Have you proofread your slides?

___ Do you need to add any slides?

___ Should you delete any slides?

___ Do you have enough handouts for everyone?

Logistics:

___ Do you know where you're going and how you're going to get there?

___ Have you gathered all the equipment and other materials you need?

___ Have you called a contact person to make sure the room will be ready?

Overcoming Nervousness

It's OK to be nervous. In fact, it's probably a good thing. If you are very calm before a presentation, you may be underestimating the difficulty of your assignment. If you're calm because you consider the topic an easy one (a "no brainer"), you may not project enough interest in your subject.

If you're not nervous, you may have a hard time projecting the energy and enthusiasm that you will need to win your listeners' attention. Nervousness can be a tool to communicate enthusiasm.

Channel your nervousness by forcing yourself to speak clearly and to make eye contact with your listeners. It cannot be stressed too often that the element of balance is important in delivering a speech.

Come across as too relaxed and you will sound a little bit bored. If you are bored, then the audience will expect to be bored as well, and they will need very little excuse to start mentally running through other things that they have to do later on that day.

Conversely, if you come across as too nervous, they will wonder why you are giving the presentation rather than someone "competent". Also remember that although eye contact with your audience is good, staring at them will just make them apprehensive – or worse yet, amused.

A Visit from the Boss

Suggested responses to statements from the boss

- I know you're going to do a great job on this presentation. *Thanks. I'm ready to go.*

- This is a very important presentation. Are you ready? *I've spent a lot of time preparing. I think it will go well.*

- You might run into some strong opposition in this meeting. *I've thought about the objections people might have and I've prepared responses.*

- Do you think you can handle this presentation? *I know what I'm going to say and what kinds of questions people will have. I'm ready.*

Sometimes even the best bosses have a tendency to put pressure on you when they would swear they are simply trying to help you. Words of encouragement may well feel as though they are loaded with other meanings.

To a nervous presenter a phrase like "I know you're going to go out there and give a great presentation" seems to be silently followed with "I know this because if you don't, I'm going to fire you at the first opportunity". This may not be what was meant, but nervousness does not always follow a logical path.

Should your boss deliver any of the above phrases of encouragement, leave aside for the time being any other meaning that they may have had. Accept their words of encouragement, and allow your boss to see that you have prepared well for the speech, and anticipate that you may run into some opposition.

As part of your preparation, you will have included your responses to any difficulties that you anticipate. Allow them to remain at the back of your mind. If you go into a presentation on the defensive, then you will find it very hard to win the approval of your audience and may even appear paranoid.

Nervousness can be energy. If it is appropriate, you may even refer to how nervous you feel and ask the audience to be gentle with you.

The work of your presentation has already mostly been done. What you are doing now is merely its culmination, so remember that you know what you are talking about, you know what you will say, and you have every right to say it.

Preparing Mentally

Some advice for participants on mental preparation:

- Like an athlete preparing for a big game, you need to keep yourself positive as you prepare for your own important contest. Think of all your successes in life – all the worthwhile things you have done. Remind yourself that you have prepared for this presentation, that you know what to expect.

- Think about similar experiences you have had. How have you responded in similar situations in the past? If you're like most people, your feelings of anxiety will gradually go away as you work your way through your presentation. You have probably been through things like this in the past – an initial period of nervousness and anxiety that lasts only a short time.

In so many cases, the anticipation of an event is the most emotionally charged part of it. The "athlete" analogy is a good one. If you allow yourself to think too much about the bad things that might happen, it becomes almost a self-fulfilling prophecy. Do not go into the meeting or conference room with a sense of foreboding and a strategy of damage limitation. All that this will do is invite problems – problems which do not need to be there.

You have already done most of the work – actually delivering the presentation is no more than the final ten per cent. Once you are in the "zone", momentum will take you to the end.

What many people actually do, and it is something that can be destructive if you allow it to be, is anticipate being nervous. The more you think "Oh, the nerves are going to get to me", the more they will. Accept that nerves are a part of public speaking, and channel those nerves into making your speech come alive.

Anyone who claims not to have been nervous the first time they spoke in public is almost certainly lying. It is something that is very hard to pre-imagine accurately, and in most cases, the nerves dissipate after the first few minutes. Accept that you will be nervous, and concentrate on delivering a good presentation. You will learn to love those nerves.

Physical Relaxation Techniques
Deep breathing:

- Sit up straight, cross your legs at the ankles or keep your feet flat on the floor.

- Take a long, slow breath in through your nose. Pretend that you are breathing into your abdomen.

- Allow your abdomen to expand.

- Exhale slowly and evenly through your nose. As you exhale, allow your abdomen to go in.

- Continue to breathe in this way for five to ten breaths.

Progressive Relaxation

- Tense a group of muscles so that they are as tightly contracted as possible.

- Hold them in this state of extreme tension for a few seconds.

- Relax the muscles as you normally would.

- Consciously relax your muscles further so that you are as relaxed as you can be.

Appearing Confident in Front of the Crowd

A speaker who fumbles around with his materials gives an impression of poor organization and lack of interest. The audience suspects that such a speaker hasn't put much effort or thought into preparing for the presentation.

Allow yourself enough time to organize all your materials before you begin your presentation. Being well-organized can also improve your self-confidence.

Remember that there is no reason for the people in the audience to feel anything but well-disposed towards you. Even if they may not agree with what you have to say, as long as you do not say it confrontationally they will accept your right to say it.

One of the most famous strategies to deal with nervousness when addressing an audience is to picture them all in their underwear. However, this is more a joke than a serious strategy. Those who have seriously tried it have found that it distracted them more than anything. It is much better simply to look out into the audience, smile in a relaxed way, and introduce yourself.

The chances are that many of your audience will smile back, and you can then address parts of your speech in their direction in order to feel supported.

The most important thing to remember in order to deliver the most confident presentation you can is to have an awareness of your surroundings. If you move around, bear in mind the positioning of things in the room. If you walk into something, pass it off with a brief joke about people planting things to put you off your stride, and simply allow your speech to flow.

Chapter 7 – Delivering Your Speech

A few simple steps can help you improve the delivery of your presentation:

- Start off strong by preparing an opening that will capture the audience's attention.

- Learn how to use visual aids effectively.

- Check the volume of your voice.

- Practice beforehand – to check running time, but not to the point where it is automatic.

As long as you have the confidence to use the room to your advantage, and have your ideas straight in your head, the presentation really will take care of itself for most of the time. You will find that, simply through saying it and hearing it often enough, your speech will evolve to a point where you can make slight adjustments on the spot as and where necessary without it becoming confusing.

Starting Off on the Right Foot

The opening of a presentation has two purposes:

- To capture the audience's attention.

- To introduce the subject of the presentation.

The opening should be very brief, in most cases one to two minutes. In that short span of time, you need to present yourself and your topic in a way that will make your audience want to pay attention. In planning your opening, go back to your analysis of your audience.

An effective opening convinces your audience that what you are going to say will be worth their time and attention. If you lose them in the first two minutes, there is not much you can do to get them back with you. In some ways the presentation's most important element is its introduction.

There are many things you can do to catch the audience's attention. Taking into account that a presentation is generally a quite formal setting, this number is maybe slightly reduced in terms of what you can do to catch the audience's attention and keep your job. However, if you work on getting the opening right, you will find that your presentations receive the attention they deserve, and that you will be able to hone them to the point where you become a very skilled presenter.

It is worth opening with a bold statement. The statement may be controversial – to the extent that it is something you believe and that some in the audience may disagree with. "Controversy" in this case is more to do with slight differences of opinion than saying something which will offend people. But it is fine to open with a statement along the lines of "X is something which is absolutely essential to the running of a business", where "X" stands for something that, up to now, many people may not have agreed was essential. Follow this up by saying "I know, many of you may not agree with me, but this is what I plan to prove to you here and now".

Making a statement which requires backing up will draw the attention of the audience, as they listen in to see how you will back it up. You will also have introduced your subject, and can then follow up with a few lines about how opinions have differed on the subject, but people with more years in the business than you have had very positive, complimentary things to say about it. In some cases, it may be beneficial to write the opening statement for your presentation after you have written the rest of it, as this allows you to make your statement chime with what you are going to say.

Using Visual Aids

Visual aids are able to:

- Clarify data that may be difficult for the audience to grasp from a verbal presentation alone. Charts and graphs are especially helpful for this purpose.

- Highlight your main ideas.

- Help your audience remember your main ideas. Many studies have shown that an audience remembers the main points of a presentation longer if the speaker uses visual aids.

- Signal transitions between major sections of your presentation.

- Shorten meetings. If handled properly, visual aids can shorten meetings by allowing the speaker to spend less time clarifying and repeating the main points of the presentation.

One study has shown that presentations that include visual aids are more persuasive than presentations that do not. There is some dispute over whether the use of visual aids is simply a gimmick to cover for the fact that a presentation does not say very much – an accusation of style over substance – and there are certainly cases where this happens.

But the coherent use of visual aids will make a presentation more memorable to the audience and will allow the presenter to make his or her points more completely. Getting it right can be difficult, but if you do get it right the pay-off can be huge.

Try to avoid simply copying the visual aids you have seen used before. If you have seen them, then the chances are that your audience will have seen them too. If they were successful then, the audience will be prone to think back to that presentation and either ignore yours or constantly compare the two.

If they were unsuccessful, then it is unlikely that they will suddenly have become more effective. It is best to think of visual aids after you have written the presentation, as this will allow you to think of a coherent uniting factor between the elements you wish to illustrate.

If you can think of a visual aid that can be used interactively, then so much the better. One obstacle which presenters find they run into is the difficulty of saying something that has not been said before, or in a way in which it has never been said.

By achieving this, you will create a situation where your audience will refer back to your presentation as "remember the time when …" Having this kind of memorable impact can make your presentation a lot more effective. It should, however, not be all that people remember. Over-reliance on visual aids will simply lead to your broader message falling on deaf ears.

Checking the Volume of Your Voice

The more people there are in a room, the louder you will have to speak. People make noise unintentionally by moving around in their seats or shuffling papers.

If you find that you have to shout to make yourself heard in the back of the room, then you need a microphone. Overall, though, conference rooms tend to be built in order to allow a presenter's voice to carry. The difficulty of getting your voice to just the right volume for a presentation is made by the fact that there are multiple rows of people viewing the presentation. In this case, it is important to take account of the seating arrangements.

Before you say anything else in a presentation, it may be a good idea to ask, in the voice you intend to use for the presentation, whether everyone can hear you clearly. The element of balance is again important here.

Speakers who are too quiet will have the obvious disadvantage that their listeners genuinely cannot hear them, as well as the fact that they will appear nervous and not in command. This does not excuse going too far in the opposite direction, which will lead people to consider you brash and over-confident, and either consciously or subconsciously give less weight to your views.

Shouting distorts the voice, and it is a simple fact that something which is shouted will not be heard as clearly as something of a similar length which is spoken powerfully from the middle of the chest. Also bear in mind that if you plan to move around the venue, you will need to make adjustments at times to ensure that your voice carries the extra distance.

If you are facing away from the audience, keep your statements during this time to a minimum, and try if possible to turn to face them during this period. If a microphone will be necessary, ensure that one is available, and tested before use – microphones can have a distorting effect which will make any presentation less worthwhile.

During the course of a presentation, you need to be aware of how things are going. Are people starting to lose interest? Do they need a break? Do you need to do something different to change the pace?

When it's time to wrap up your presentation, you need to remind people of your basic message. You hope that a week from now, if someone asked the members of your audience they would be able to recall what your presentation was all about.

This is something that depends greatly upon the audience, but as you have no control over their reactions your job is simply to ensure that you get your message across as persuasively as you possibly can.

You will probably be given an allotted time to deliver your presentation, and it is a good idea to take this time and look at all the elements you need to cover. By doing this you can then divide the allotted time into shorter spells in which you can cover the topics in hand.

Adjusting on the Fly

Here are some adjustments you could make if the audience seemed to be losing interest:

- Ask questions.

- Have a member of the audience come to the front of the room and help you with a demonstration.

- Conduct an informal poll ("How many people think that…?").

- Introduce a brief, interesting digression (go off topic for two or three minutes).

- Use a brief anecdote (preferably one that has something to do with your topic).

Each of the above adjustments has the advantage of offering a change of pace, and if your audience has given the appearance of losing interest these can turn that around by reminding the audience that there is a reason for them to listen.

Some audiences react to different things than others, and you will normally be able to tell what it is that your presentation lacks by reading the faces of your audience. If they look slightly pained and confused, it may be that you are speaking from a vocabulary with which they are unfamiliar. If they simply look bored, then it may be that you are not telling them anything new.

Involving the audience is something which, done carefully, can get a presentation right back on track when it has been threatening to lose their attention. From something as simple as not wanting to be called up to the front and exposed for their failure to pay attention, to something as enjoyable as the ability to participate in a genuinely interesting diversion, this will cause people to sit forward and become more interested in proceedings.

It may also be that you have been speaking excessively formally, and have appeared distanced and humorless. Obviously, a lot has gone into this presentation and you may well consider it to be "no laughing matter", but a certain lightness of touch can make the presentation flow better and involve the audience more. It is wise to avoid disrespectful humor, but some light self-mocking can go a long way to getting the audience on your side.

Gauging Whether Breaks Are Required

When you tell people to take a break, tell them exactly when you plan to start again. Fifteen minutes is a typical length for a break. The shorter presentations – those under an hour, will generally not require a break, but if the presentation edges towards an hour and a half it may well be that offering a break in the middle can be the wisest thing to do.

Although people will sit for upwards of two hours in a movie theater, there is a clear difference between a movie and a presentation. Atmospherically, dynamically and in many other ways it is much easier to sit through a film of a certain length than it is to sit through a presentation of the same length.

If you do give a break to the audience at a presentation, it is essential to specify that you will begin the presentation again at a set time and impress upon them the importance of their being back at the right time.

If people stay out beyond the allotted time for a break then it simply results in the recommencing of the presentation being delayed, and gives a very bad impression. If there are some stragglers who take a little bit more time to arrive back, then it is beneficial to simply have a short, informal conversation with the people who have arrived on time or stayed in the auditorium during the break.

This can be a good way of gauging how the presentation is being received, and allow you to get an impression for what your audience is like.

Wrapping Up and Winding Down

Sometimes a speaker will end a presentation with a question and answer session. If you do this, don't end the presentation with your answer to the last question. It might have little to do with your main point. Instead, after you have answered the last question, say something like:

"That's all we have time for. If there is one thing I hope you will remember from this presentation, it's..."

Doing this will end the presentation in a neat way, and pull together the strands of the previous period of time. It will also allow you to reinforce the central point of your presentation. As people leave, thank them for attending and say goodbye to them.

If people leave the presentation on a positive note they are more likely to remember what has gone before in a positive light. Whatever else you do, you should ensure that if people have follow-up questions after the event they can address them to you in whatever way is possible.

Questions and Answers

The way you respond to questions will have a major effect on what kind of rapport you are able to build with the audience. If you answer questions thoughtfully and respectfully, people will feel that you are taking them seriously. If you give flip, dismissive answers, people will feel that you don't have time for them.

People may ask questions which are not a hundred per cent serious, but even then you should not be dismissive, simply take the question in the spirit it was intended and take the opportunity to display a sense of humor.

Questions may well be an opportunity for you to get information into the presentation that you could not address due to overall time constraints. When someone asks a good question, begin your response with a sentence along the lines of *"That's a very good question, and I am glad you asked me that. I think the most important thing here is that..."*

If someone asks a question which you find either you cannot answer or which is difficult, do not simply say *"I don't know"* but say *"That's a good question. I have to admit I hadn't covered that issue – what do you think?"* This way you will not lose respect, but will allow discussion to flow more freely.

Ground Rules

At the end of your presentation you say, "Does anyone have any questions?" And no one does. What do you do? You could try waiting for 20 seconds or so and then say, "Well, one question people often ask is…" Come up with your own question to show people what kinds of questions you expect.

NOTE: The question you come up with should be an easy one so people will get the idea that they don't have to ask something very complicated or difficult.

If the presentation is longer than an hour, it is beneficial to allow questions at regular intervals. This is because the longer people are sat in silence, the less interest they will show in whatever is at hand.

However, most presentations will be shorter than that, and it is advisable to hold off questions until the end. If you have an hour in total for the presentation, you should look to wind down at the 45-minute mark and take questions in the last fifteen minutes.

This will allow you to answer questions and look for feedback on those answers. An open question-and-answer session will enliven matters with more group participation. It will give everyone a chance to participate – in a way which will reinforce what they hopefully have learned.

Answering Questions That Sound Like an Attack

At some point, someone in your audience might ask a question that sounds like an attack. How should you respond to a hostile question?

Don't confront the person. Don't say, *"No, I think you're wrong."*

Affirm the person. Say,

"That's an interesting point, but here's another way to look at."

"I can see why you would feel that way, but I was trying to make the point that..."

"Point taken; I might have been too sweeping in my generalization."

Everyone in the room will be waiting to hear how you respond to the challenge. If you keep cool and say something positive before you proceed to your answer, you will impress your audience with your professionalism and your command of the situation.

Agree with the person as far as you can. State your disagreement in a non-confrontational way. *"I think we agree on XYX, but not on ABC."*

Answering hostile questions with an equally hostile response will simply make the whole process tense. As you are the person at the front of the room, and the person asking the question is sat with a number of other people, it will simply set you against a larger group of people, making the atmosphere needlessly confrontational.

Additionally, if you answer a hostile question by showing good grace and considering the question on its positive merits, you will increase the likelihood of the initially hostile individual backing down from their confrontational position, whether through embarrassment for their unnecessary hostility, or because they were impressed by you looking to answer their question fairly despite the fact that it could have been taken as an attack.

It should be clear that you are not a teacher to the group of people, but some of the principles of teaching remain intact. Among these, the fact that you are in a position of some responsibility and importance should prevent you from allowing yourself to have a pop back at the person.

Dealing with Complex Questions

Listen

- Listen attentively to the question.

- Make eye contact with the questioner.

- Nod or give other indications of encouragement.

- Don't interrupt.

- Paraphrase when appropriate. If a person asks a long, rambling question, you might want to paraphrase it before you respond. Say something like, *"Let me be sure I understand you. You are asking..."*

Analyze

- Before responding, make sure you understand the question.

- Try to determine the intent of the questioner. Is he genuinely asking for clarification, or is he trying to disprove or challenge you? Watch facial expression and body language. Listen for tone.

- Ask yourself; is there a broader issue behind the question that I need to address?

Affirm

- Make eye contact with the questioner again.

- Say something like, *"That's an interesting point,"* or *"I'm glad you brought that up."* An affirmation of this kind is especially important if the question was asked in a challenging way.

Answer

- Don't duck a question or give a vague answer.

- If you don't know the answer, say so. You might want to tell the questioner that you will call him the next day with an answer.

- Give an honest answer. If the audience gets the impression that you are trying to put one over on them, you might as well pack up and go home.

The question and answer session traditionally comes at the end of the presentation, so if you shine during this section, people will remember that very clearly, as they will surely remember you negatively if you duck questions or give fraudulent answers. Ending on a positive note is hugely important in a presentation, and if you can do that you are most of the way to being a good public speaker.

Additional Titles

The 90 Minute Guide series of books covers a variety of general business skills and are intended to be completed in 90 minutes or less. It is an effective way for building your skill set and can be used to acquire professional development units needed by project managers and other industries to maintain their certification. For the availability of titles please see

https://www.silvercitypublications.com/shop/.

No. 1 - Appreciative Inquiry

No. 2 - Assertiveness and Self Control

No. 3 - Attention Management

No. 4 - Body Language Basics

No. 5 - Business Acumen

No. 6 - Business and Etiquette

No. 7 - Change Management

No. 8 - Coaching and Mentoring

No. 9 - Communications Strategies

No. 10 - Conflict Resolution